coast-to-coast games

Contents

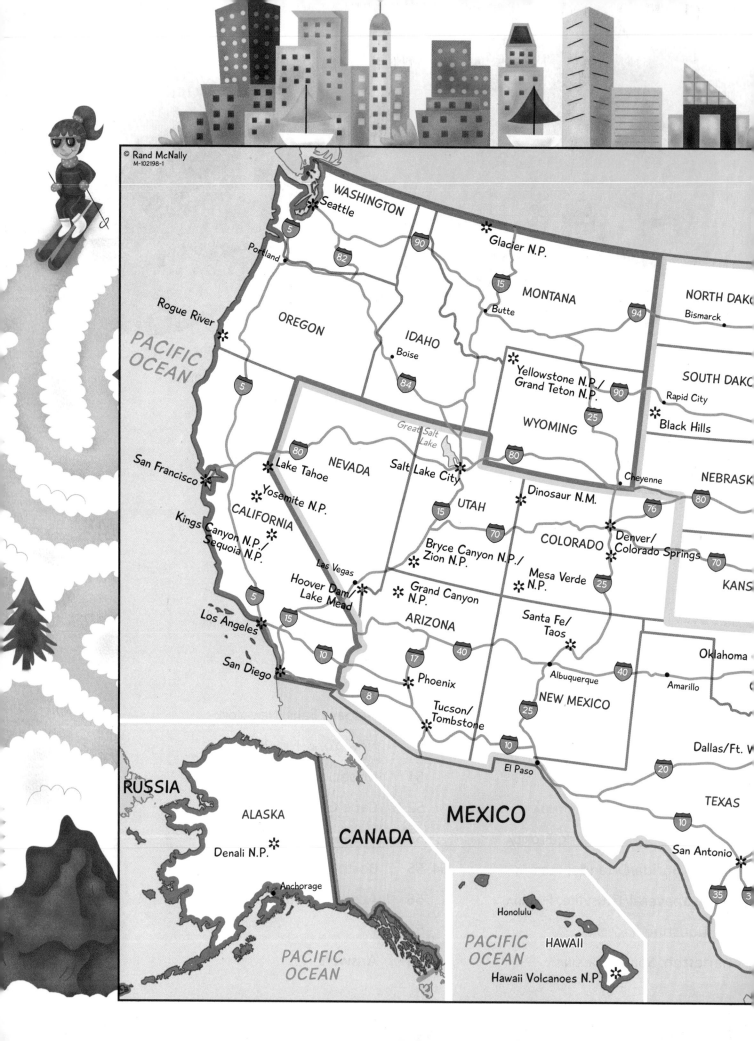

© Rand McNally
M-102198-1

WASHINGTON

*Seattle

Portland

PACIFIC
OCEAN

Rogue River

OREGON

IDAHO

Boise

90

82

*Glacier N.P.

15

MONTANA

Butte

94

NORTH DAKO

Bismarck

SOUTH DAKO

84

Great Salt
Lake

80

NEVADA

*Lake Tahoe

Salt Lake City

*Yosemite N.P.

CALIFORNIA

Kings Canyon N.P./
Sequoia N.P.

Las Vegas

Hoover Dam/
Lake Mead

San Francisco

5

Los Angeles

10

15

San Diego

8

*Yellowstone N.P./
Grand Teton N.P.

90

Rapid City

*Black Hills

WYOMING

80

Cheyenne

15

UTAH

*Dinosaur N.M.

76

NEBRASK

80

70

COLORADO

*Denver/
Colorado Springs

70

*Bryce Canyon N.P./
Zion N.P.

*Mesa Verde
N.P.

25

KANS

*Grand Canyon
N.P.

ARIZONA

17

40

Santa Fe/
Taos

Oklahoma

Amarillo

*Phoenix

Albuquerque

40

Tucson/
Tombstone

NEW MEXICO

25

Dallas/Ft. W

10

El Paso

20

RUSSIA

ALASKA

*Denali N.P.

Anchorage

CANADA

MEXICO

TEXAS

10

San Antonio

35

3

PACIFIC
OCEAN

Honolulu

PACIFIC
OCEAN

HAWAII

Hawaii Volcanoes N.P.

CANADA

MINNESOTA
Duluth
35
94
WISCONSIN
90
43
eapolis/
St. Paul
Wisconsin Dells
Milwaukee
Lake Superior
Lake Michigan
Lake Huron
MICHIGAN
75
Dearborn
94
Detroit
Lake Erie
90
Cleveland
IOWA
80
Chicago
80
90
OHIO
77
PENNSYLVANIA
80
Pittsburgh
Valley
Forge
NEW
YORK
81
90
87
Lake Ontario
88
Niagara
Falls
74
ILLINOIS
65
69
75
70
76
Lancaster
MAINE
95
Arcadia N.P.
VT.
89
N.H.
Portland
Boston
Plymouth
Cape Cod
MASS.
CONN.
R.I.
Mystic
New York
NEW JERSEY
Philadelphia
57
Indianapolis
71
WEST
VIRGINIA
79
68
Washington
D.C.
MARYLAND
DELAWARE
Baltimore
35
INDIANA
74
Cincinnati
55
MISSOURI
70
City
9
St. Louis
49
Louisville
64
Bluegrass
Country
KENTUCKY
Mammoth
Cave N.P.
24
81
64
Richmond
VIRGINIA
85
Williamsburg
Jamestown
Cape Hatteras
ATLANTIC
OCEAN
44
Ozarks
40
Little
Rock
40
ARKANSAS
Nashville
TENNESSEE
Great Smoky
Mtns. N.P.
75
40
NORTH
CAROLINA
95
Charlotte
30
55
65
59
Huntsville
Atlanta
20
26
SOUTH
CAROLINA
Charleston
MISSISSIPPI
20
85
GEORGIA
16
20
Natchez
49
59
ALABAMA
65
LOUISIANA
10
10
New
Orleans
10
95
St. Augustine
Cape Kennedy/
Titusville
75
Central Florida/
Orlando
4
Tampa/
St. Petersburg
FLORIDA
95
Miami
Everglades N.P.
BAHAMAS
N
GULF OF MEXICO

Guide to Adventure
Symbols
✳ Terrific Place
• City
Regions
Middle Atlantic
Midwest
Northeast
Pacific Coast &
Northern Rocky Mountains
South
Southwest
Abbreviations
N.P. National Park
N.M. National Monument

With *Coast-to-Coast Games* you can discover exciting new adventures, coast to coast and border to border within the United States. Check out the great scenery and terrific things to see and do, and meet some interesting people. It's time to explore these fun kid-friendly places along the way.

This book will tell you about many of these places. Read a little, play the games, and pretend that you are there. The United States map at the beginning of this book will show you where these places are located. Look into the ones that are near your home, or plan to visit the places that seem fun to you. Be sure to watch for the little red bird throughout this book for special surprises.

The travel games will make the time fly as you ride along in the car or fly in an airplane. Play the games alone or with other people. The games range from easy to hard but all of them are fun. The only supplies you need are a pencil, crayons, and coins or other markers.

So grab your book and supplies, buckle up, and you're off on a great adventure "coast to coast."

Hawaii's Volcanoes

Look into a volcano at Hawaii Volcanoes National Park and imagine how the world looked long ago. Stand at the rim—but be careful! Down below a fiery pit glows with power...black lava rock twists its way through a strange, bare land...and puffs of evil-smelling steam escape from cracks in the ground.

Did You Know?
The big island of Hawaii is the youngest of the present Hawaiian islands. But, to the southeast of Hawaii, under the water, is a new volcanic island forming which should reach the surface in about 10,000 years.

Can you identify the parts of a volcano?

Cinder cone_____   Lava_____

Crater_____   Magma_____

Eruption_____   Vent_____

Gas and ash_____   Volcanic bombs_____

7

Denali National Park

Alaska

Where's the highest mountain in North America? Right here! Mt. McKinley is so tall (20,320 feet) that its peak is nearly always covered by clouds. Walking on the tundra feels strange—it's bouncy. Don't forget to bring binoculars to spy on the grizzly bears and other wild animals.

Midnight Sun!

Find and circle these things you can see in Denali.

Arctic Warbler	Marmot
Bear	Moose
Beaver	Mountain Goat
Caribou	Mount McKinley
Cliff	Otter
Cub	Pika
Dall Sheep	Ptarmigan
Fox	Raven
Glacier	River
Golden Eagle	Rock
Golden Plover	Snow Bunting
Grebe	Snowshoe Hare
Grizzly Bear	Spruce
Hill	Squirrel
Ice	Tern
Log	Valley
Long-Tailed Jaeger	Wheatear
Loon	Wolf
Lynx	Wolverine

```
L O O N G G N I T N U B W O N S
L O N N A G I M R A T P O W P R
E O N R A S Q U I R R E L H E T
Y N G G E O R E V I R L V E E A
E R R O T T E R A T I T E A H R
L E E Y L A H K E H A R R T S C
N L B E N D I E S O O M I E L T
I G E L A P E L G D R N N A L I
K A L L E V E N E M F E E R A C
C E R A E C I U P D A F V V D W
M N A V C A U C O L J R I A A A
T E E F T I U R Y B O A M L E R
N D B N L B E N P N I V E O C B
U L U T F O X R U S R R E G T L
O O E S N O W S H O E H A R E E
M G R I Z Z L Y B E A R O C K R
```

Ever eat in a moving restaurant? There are two of them at the top of the 605-foot Space Needle. Look down on the city, then get down and explore the tide pools, astro-space displays, and more at the Pacific Science Center. Ride the monorail downtown, eat your way through Pike Place Market, then take a boat ride around Puget Sound.

Seattle
Washington

Waterfront Wonders!
See the Seattle waterfront's great scenery, sights and shopping. Four miles long, start at either end.

7 **Waterfront Park–**
Fishing, scenery, picnicking

8 **The Seattle Aquarium–**
Dome puts you underwater for a fish-eye view

9 **Pike Street Hillclimb–**
157 steps up to fascinating...

19 **Pike Place Market–**
Longest continuously operating farmers' market in the U.S.

1 **King Street Station–**
Historic train station

2 **Klondike Gold Rush National Historical Park–**
See things needed by miners heading to the Klondike gold fields in Alaska and Canada in 1897–98

3 **Pioneer Square–**
Heart of Old Seattle; see the totem pole

4 **Washington State Ferry Terminal–**
Ferries leave for many places including Canada

5 **Seattle Harbor Tours–**
Take a tour of the harbor, Pier 55

6 **Pier 56–**
Tours to Tillicum Indian Village at Blake Island State Park

START

9

Rogue River

Oregon

Black bears, river otters, and bald eagles hunt and play along the Rogue River. Look for them as you travel this wild, watery, "road." You might choose to bounce through the tumbling water in a rubber raft. Or would you rather roar and splash your way upstream in a jet boat?

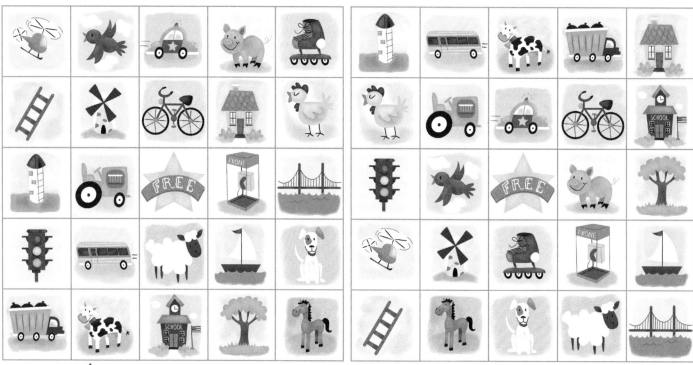

Backseat Bingo!

As you ride along, when you see one of these things, mark the picture square on your card. If you see a horse, mark the square with a horse on it. To play alone, pretend you are playing with a friend, and see who wins. The first filled row of squares diagonally, up and down, or across is the winner.

Glacier National Park

Want to make snowballs in summer? In this park, summer isn't just for flowers. Snow lays scattered over the ground all year. Huge rivers of ice called glaciers creep over the land, slower than a snail. Hike the trails and try to spot bighorn sheep or mountain goats before they spot you.

Montana

Stash your trash!

The national parks are our wonderful heritage. Lets keep them clean and beautiful. Draw a line from each item to its environmental lifetime.

1 month

3 months

200-500 years

Over 500 years

As much as 1,000,000 years, (maybe never!)

Yellowstone/Grand Teton National Parks

Wyoming

The oldest national park has...Old Faithful! This famous geyser shoots water more than a hundred feet into the air. Mudpots pop and plop their oozy contents out like little volcanoes. And hot springs spread out like spilled paint—bright blue, green, orange, and yellow. Look out for the bears!

Hot Stuff!

Do you know what to look for in Yellowstone Park? Crack the code to see!

YOZXP YVZI_____

TVBHVIH_____

YRHLM_____

NZNNLGS SLG HKIRMTH_____

TIRAAOB YVZI_____

NLLHV_____

VOP (DZKRGR)_____

ZMGVOLKV_____

YRTSLIM HSVVK_____

BVOOLDHGLMV UZOOH_____

YZOW VZTOV_____

LOW UZRGSUFO_____

KZRMG KLGH_____

YVZEVI_____

A	B	C	D	E	F	G	H	I	J	K	L	M
Z	Y	X	W	V	U	T	S	R	Q	P	O	N

N	O	P	Q	R	S	T	U	V	W	X	Y	Z
M	L	K	J	I	H	G	F	E	D	C	B	A

Grand Teton National Park

Time for some exercise! Hiking and mountain climbing are the best ways to enjoy the wild scenery of this park. Keep an eye out for moose—they're everywhere. When you're tired or just for fun, relax with a float trip on the Snake River. Or, take a boat ride around Jackson Lake. In Jackson Hole, in the winter skiing is great and it is fun to watch the huge local elk herd check in for a free lunch.

Riddle Time!

What has banks, but no money?_____

What has legs, but can't walk?_____

What has eyes, but can't see?_____

What has a bed, but never sleeps?_____

What has arms, but can't hug?_____

What has hands, but can't clap?_____

What has a face, but no head?_____

What has a mouth, but never smiles?_____

What has heels, but no feet?_____

What has a head and foot, but no body?_____

What has a neck, but no head?_____

What has an elbow, but no arm?_____

What has knees, but no legs?_____

What has ears, but can't hear?_____

What has fingers, but can't type?_____

Lake Tahoe

Boat or "fly," sail or slide. This mountain lake is fun to visit year round. In the summer, hit the beaches for swimming, boating, or parasailing. In the winter, head for the mountain slopes surrounding Lake Tahoe. The snow is deep and the skiing is great!

California

Nevada

What Can You Do at Lake Tahoe?

Fill in the fun activities from the clues. When you finish, the letters in the boxes will tell you where you are.

_ _ □ _   Played with a club and small ball

_ _ _ _ □ _ _   Glide on an ice rink

_ _ □ _   Downhill or cross-country

_ _ _ □ _ _   Gallop on a horse

□ _ _ _ _ _   You need a racket, ball, and net

_ _ □ _ _   Go in a boat without a motor

_ □ _ _   A walk in the outdoors

_ _ □ _   Rides on the water

_ _ _ □ _ _ _   Ride on the water behind a boat

Did You Know?

Lake Tahoe, a magnificent emerald-colored mountain lake located in two states, is 6,229 feet high, up to 1,640 feet deep, and 193 square miles in area.

Roller coaster up and down the city hills on the cable cars. Wiggle your way along Lombard Street, the most twisty street in the world. Find chicken feet for sale in Chinatown and crabs at Fisherman's Wharf. Explore museums and an aquarium in Golden Gate Park, or the old prison on Alcatraz Island.

San Francisco

Did You Know?

The Golden Gate Bridge:
- is not gold but red
- has towers 746 feet high
- has a 4,200-foot main span
- is 1.7 miles long (8,981 feet)
- has main support cables 3 feet in diameter
- needs 60,000 gallons of paint to paint it

California

Hit the Road!

If you are traveling on I-80 from New York City to San Francisco, through how many states will you pass?_____

What are they? Use the map on pages 4 and 5.

_____ _____
_____ _____
_____ _____
_____ _____
_____

Yosemite National Park

Look up and up and up! Everything here is taller than tall. The rock cliffs and peaks push at the sky. Waterfalls look as if they are falling from the clouds. Even the trees are huge—especially the Grizzly Giant! The Pioneer History Center and the Indian Museum bring back the olden days.

All Aboard!

Yosemite is full of wonderful things to see and do. Fill in the puzzle to learn what some of them are.

Nut	Canyon
Fern	Meadow
Hike	Merced
Lake	Camping
Pass	Sequoia
Peak	Sierras
Roam	Ahwahnee
Rock	Half Dome
Tree	Mariposa
Vale	Mountain
View	Tuolumne
Eagle	Edyth Lake
Trail	El Capitan
	Yosemite Falls

California

Tree Ring Circus!

Some of California's trees are very big and very old. Count the rings of each of these trees to tell how old. Which two tree sections are from the same tree? Don't forget to count the middle.

You'll feel as small as an ant when you walk through the giant forest of sequoia trees (named for the Indian chief Sequoyah). The General Sherman tree is the largest living tree in the world—taller than a 25-story building. You can also see a real cabin built in a hollow log and tour Crystal Cave.

HOLLYWOOD

Los Angeles

California

You can quiver through an earthquake at Universal Studios and meet Mickey Mouse at Disneyland. See tar pits that trapped prehistoric beasts. Shop at a Mexican street market in Old Los Angeles. Visit Griffith Park to roam the zoo, ride a merry-go-round, or see stars in the planetarium.

Cars, cars, and more cars!
Fill in these words that begin with C A R.

C A R __ __ __ __   A chewy treat

C A R __ __ __   Seeds found in rye bread

C A R __ __ __ __ __ __ __ __   Part of a car's engine

C A R __ __   There are 52 in a deck

C A R __ __ __ __ __   A bright red bird

C A R __ __ __ __   Watch out!

C A R __ __ __ __ __   Lots of rides and fun

C A R __ __ __ __ __   Merry-go-round

C A R __ __ __ __ __ __ __   He works with a hammer and nails

C A R __ __ __   A large rug

C A R __ __ __ __ __   Babies ride in style

C A R __ __ __   A rabbit's favorite food

C A R __ __ __   A cardboard box

STUDIO 5B

Round and Round She Goes!

Hop aboard the ferris wheel to discover things to see in Los Angeles. The letters you need to crack the code are red.

TJOYRCDZYT   _____

FYWMM'O XRQQC   _____
   PZQB   _____

LWDDCGWWT   _____

PZQBRQ'O BZQFRM   _____

ORZ GWQDT   _____

QZYVLW DZ XQRZ MZQ _____
   UJMO   _____

LWDDCGWWT XWGD _____

OJE PDZNO BZNJV _____
   BWKYMZJY

KYJIRQOZD OMKTJWO _____
   LWDDCGWWT   _____

SKRRY BZQC   _____

XRIRQDC LJDDO   _____

QWOR XWGD   _____

NRYR ZKMQC GROMRQY _____
   LRQJMZNR BKORKB _____

YXV OMKTJWO   _____

NQJPPJML UZQF
   WXORQIZMWQC _____

MLR VWDJORKB   _____

19

San Diego

California

Have fun that's wet and wild! Look a shark in the eye and feed a dolphin at Sea World, or hit the beaches. Explore a jungle at the zoo, and watch wild animals on the loose at the Wild Animal Park. If you like planes, trains, dinosaurs, or science, check out the fun at the museums in Balboa Park.

Do the Zoo, San Diego That Is!

Who has the longest neck?

Who has the longest nose?

Who can run the fastest?

Who is the King of the Beasts?

Who is the horse in striped pajamas?

Who can hang by his tail?

Who comes with her own pocket?

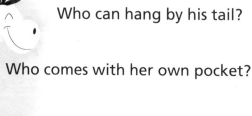

Who is called a river horse?

Utah

Bob like a beach ball in the Great Salt Lake or catch the waves at Raging Water theme park. For games, rides and other fun, head for the 49th Street Galleria. Time travel back to pioneer days with a visit to Old Deseret Village or count the organ pipes at the Mormon Tabernacle. Look for the Seagull Monument. This bird is very special to the city.

Capital Place!

How much do you know about our state capitals? Try this quiz and see!

1. What two state names are found in the names of their state capitals?

2. In which state capital is the U.S. Naval Academy located?

3. What capital name means "red stick" in French?

4. What state capital is named for our 16th president?

5. Which state capital is known as "Music City?"

6. What four states and their capitals begin with the same letter?

7. Which state capital can <u>only</u> be reached by plane or boat?

8. Name six state capitals that begin with "s."

9. Which state capital has the longest history?

10. Which state capital means stone in French?

Did You Know?

The Great Salt Lake is the second saltiest body of water in the world, after the Dead Sea, between 6 and 27 percent salt. Makes floating very easy!

Dinosaur National Monument

This park is really Jurassic! Well, the dinosaurs don't move, but you will find more Jurassic-age dinosaur bones, skulls, and skeletons here than anywhere else in the world. There are also weird land formations caused by the wind and rain eating away at the earth. Perfect for a dinosaur park!

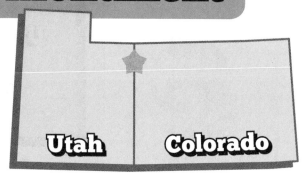

Utah | Colorado

Make No Bones About It!

At this park more than 2,000 dinosaur bones are exposed on a wall inside the park building. Can you find the six dinosaurs that are hiding outside?

Utah

Bryce Canyon/Zion National Parks

Castles, people, chessmen, a box of giant stone crayons...All kinds of strange shapes can be seen in the white, purple, pink, red, orange, and yellow rocks that fill Bryce Canyon National Park. At Zion, earn a patch from the Junior Ranger program. Also check out the hanging gardens and Weeping Rock.

Rocky Road!

These two parks have beautiful and fun things to see. Find and circle them in the puzzle below.

Bike	Hike	Sun
Bryce	Lore	Top
Camp	Red	Tower
Canyon	Ride	Wall
Cliff	Rim	Zion
Fold	Rock	

```
E K C L I F F
K C A M P O T
I O N W A L L
B R Y C E D O
Z I O N D E R
S U N H I K E
T O W E R I M
```

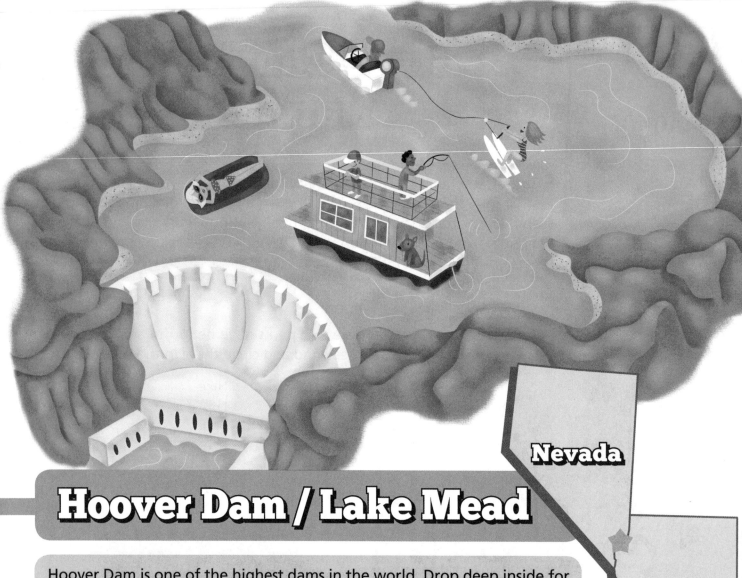

Hoover Dam / Lake Mead

Nevada

Arizona

Hoover Dam is one of the highest dams in the world. Drop deep inside for a tour with a 44-story elevator ride and you still won't be at the bottom. Then, find a spot on Lake Mead to boat, fish, swim, or waterski. There's plenty of room—it's the biggest man-made lake in the United States.

Rhyme Time!
Find the rhyming answers to each pair of riddles.

It blocks a river_____
A baby sheep_____

You walk on them_____
A large red vegetable_____

A round toy_____
Great place to shop_____

They tell the time_____
Baby toys with letters_____

It has an on/off switch_____
A dog and cat may do this_____

Finger jewelry_____
Kids like to do this_____

A smile is found on this_____
Opposite of north_____

Fun to read_____
Make dinner_____

It has two wheels_____
A walk in the woods_____

Frogs like to_____
Gasoline comes out of a_____

Grand Canyon National Park

Arizona

This is one big ditch! Stand on the South Rim of the Grand Canyon, and you'll be looking a mile down and almost 10 miles across. For a different view, look up at the massive canyon walls from a raft plunging on the Colorado River. Or, ride a mule into the canyon past the colorful, layered cliffs.

Some View!

Hop aboard a mule and ride down into the Grand Canyon. See if you can find the way.

Phoenix

Want to walk through a forest of cacti? Visit the Desert Botanical Garden where mighty saguaro cacti stand at attention like prickly crossing guards. Phoenix also has a Doll and Toy Museum, the Pueblo Grande Indian Museum, and a Mystery Castle built of desert rocks.

Arizona

Prickly Place!

Deserts have beautiful cacti, wildflower, and desert plants. Color these that are found in Arizona. Saguaro's big arms have white and yellow flowers. Pink flowers crown the short, round, gray-green pincushion. Bear grass is bushy with a tall white flower. Red blossoms tip the ocotillo's long, thin branches. Prickly pear has flat, thick leaves with golden flowers. Orange blooms top the barrel cactus. Joshua tree branches have green, prickly, bushy ends. Hedgehog has dark pink blossoms.

O.K. CORRAL

Tucson / Tombstone

Arizona

Tarantulas and rattlesnakes are among the critters that hang out at the Tucson-Sonora Desert Museum—really a kind of zoo. Watch Wild West shoot-outs at Old Tucson Studios. See the graves of real Old West outlaws and lawmen on Boot Hill in nearby Tombstone. For a look at the future, stop by Biosphere 2.

Shop Till You Drop!
Shopping is always fun. Where can you find these cool souvenirs?

Arizona-Sonora Desert Museum _____

Barrio Historico _____

Fort Huachuca _____

Kitt Peak Observatory _____

O.K. Corral _____

Old Tucson _____

Pima Air Museum _____

Tombstone _____

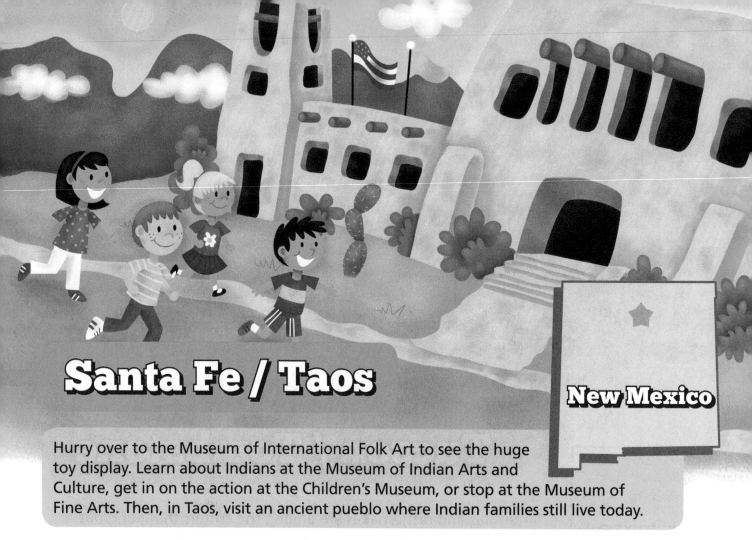

Santa Fe / Taos

New Mexico

Hurry over to the Museum of International Folk Art to see the huge toy display. Learn about Indians at the Museum of Indian Arts and Culture, get in on the action at the Children's Museum, or stop at the Museum of Fine Arts. Then, in Taos, visit an ancient pueblo where Indian families still live today.

Ancient Apartment House!

Taos Indians have lived here for 1,000 years, many of those years in this pueblo. Color the scene with bright cheerful colors.

Mesa Verde means "green table" in Spanish, and that's just what this huge, forest-covered rock platform looks like. But it's a table with a secret. From the top, peer down into canyons and discover ancient Indian homes built on huge shelves high in the sides of the cliff. A golden stone city waiting to be explored.

Colorado

Mesa Verde

Pick a Path!

Start up the ladder and wind your way through the ruins on one of the two paths that lead to Balcony House or follow another path to the Kiva.

KIVA

BALCONY HOUSE

Denver/Colorado Springs

Maybe your allowance came from Denver—check out the United States Mint where lots of our coins are made. Don't just admire the mountains, climb to the top of Colorado Springs' Pikes Peak by road or cog railway, or spy on Kissing Camels in the Garden of the Gods. P.S. The skiing is great! If you like amusement parks, head for Elitch Gardens.

Colorado

Awesome! Find the right ski trail to the bottom of Pikes Peak.

LODGE

Oklahoma City/Tulsa

Oil wells? Cowboy statues? Giant talking money? Oklahoma City has it all! Check out the Capital building, the Cowboy Hall of Fame, and Enterprise Square USA. In Tulsa, you can shop at a real Indian trading post, then head to Allen Ranch for a horseback ride, hay ride, and chuckwagon supper.

Oklahoma

Tribal Tracking!
Follow the Indian trail. Find 20 things that begin with a "t."

Did You Know?
Oklahoma has the only state capitol with oil wells on the lawn and in the basement. In Tulsa, the Gilcrease Museum, one of the world's finest Western art collections, was founded by Thomas Gilcrease, a man of Creek Indian descent who made his fortune in oil.

Dallas/Fort Worth

Cheer the bucking bronco or yell "Ride 'em cowboy!" at a real western rodeo. Investigate pioneer life at Log Cabin Village in Fort Worth or Old City Park in Dallas. The days of cattle drives come alive at the Fort Worth stockyards. For modern-day excitement, there's Six Flags Over Texas.

Texas

Catch This!
Study for one minute these items you would use to play sports. Close the book. See how many you can remember.

Explore by foot...or by boat! A river runs right through downtown. Downtown is also where you'll find that famous Spanish mission (and battle site) the Alamo, a Mexican market, and lots of great museums. When you need a history break, cheer on the watery stars at Sea World of Texas.

San Antonio

Texas

Buena Suerte!

San Antonio has lots of Spanish atmosphere. Identify these Spanish words from the scene below.

arbol ____   burro ____   casa ____   gato ____   iglesia ____   mano ____

niña ____   niño ____   pelo ____   pelota ____   perro ____   piñata ____

serape ____   sol ____   sombrero ____   zapatos ____

33

Black Hills

South Dakota

This is gold country! Grab a pan and sift for nuggets like an old-time prospector, or tour a mine. Haunt a ghost town, or prowl caves filled with jewel-like crystals. Chug the tracks in an 1880 steam train. At Mt. Rushmore you'll see presidents with noses almost as long as a school bus!

Gold Mining!
Find the six hidden things about the Black Hills.

Scenic Stumpers!

How about a game to help enjoy the scenery? Play this with several people, or it can be played alone.

1. The first player picks something from the passing scene.

2. The next person has to name something that begins with the last letter of the first item.

3. Try to stump the other players by picking something with an unusual last letter (for example "X").

4. If all are stumped by your word, you get to start the next game.

Black Hills Trivia

- Gold comes in many different colors.
- The heads on Mt. Rushmore are 60 feet from forehead to chin and took 14 years to carve.
- There are many beautiful caves to visit beneath the Black Hills.
- Bison bulls weigh nearly a ton and can run faster than a horse.
- Custer State Park has many bison and some famous begging burros.
- You can still pan for gold today in the Black Hills, in Deadwood, Lead, and Hill City.
- Wooly mammoths once lived around Hot Spings in the Black Hills.

Minneapolis / St. Paul

Minnesota

Don't worry about the weather here. Glass skyways connect the downtown buildings—a hamster maze for humans! There are also lakes for swimming, fishing, and boating. Hope aboard for a sternwheeler ride on the Mississippi River; or explore a fort, two zoos, and an outdoor sculpture park (check out the giant cherry).

Cruisin' Down the River!

If you were Tom Sawyer or Huck Finn floating down the Mississippi River on a raft, what states would you pass on your travels?

Start at the arrow and write every other letter until you have gone around the circle twice, filling in the blanks.

M _ _ _ _ _ _ _ _

I _ _ _ _

M _ _ _ _ _ _ _

A _ _ _ _ _ _ _ _

L _ _ _ _ _ _ _ _ _

W _ _ _ _ _ _ _ _ _

I _ _ _ _ _ _ _

K _ _ _ _ _ _ _

T _ _ _ _ _ _ _ _

M _ _ _ _ _ _ _ _ _ _

"Wet" is the word for the Dells! Ride a duck (a special car, not a quacker) over land *and* water. Take a boat tour through narrow canyons and past weird rock formations. Pick a water park to splash and play, or watch a waterski show. Time to dry off? How about a wild round of miniature golf, or enter the future at the Tommy Bartlett Exploratory.

What a Wild Waterslide!
When Mary jumps in, where will she come out? Tube 1, 2, or 3?

Wisconsin

Milwaukee

Walk through a rain forest or meet face-to-face with life-size dinosaurs at the Public Museum. Then, experiment with science at Discovery World. After a stop at the terrific zoo, wander through the Domes. These round plant museums are HUGE! Each is almost half a foodball field wide and seven stories tall.

Wisconsin

Whose lunch?
Lunches got all mixed up at the zoo. Help each animal find its own lunch. Draw a line to join the right pairs.

For an eagle's-eye view of the city, soar to the top of Willis Tower—the world's tallest building. Watch whales at the Shedd Aquarium, climb through a coal mine at the Museum of Science and Industry, or enter an Egyptian tomb at the Field Museum. Then, go ape with the gorillas at Lincoln Park Zoo.

Chicago

Illinois

Great Shape!
If you try, you can see other shapes in several of the Great Lakes. Identify the lakes that have shapes like these.

LAKE SUPERIOR

MICH.

WISCONSIN

LAKE MICHIGAN

LAKE HURON

CANADA

MICHIGAN

LAKE ONTARIO

NEW YORK

LAKE ERIE

PENNSYLVANIA

ILLINOIS

INDIANA

OHIO

Did You Know?
Combine the first letters of the names of the Great Lakes to spell HOMES. It will help you remember them (Huron, Ontario, Michigan, Erie, Superior).

Dearborn

Michigan

American sights and sounds fill the Henry Ford Museum. Find cars and comics, eggbeaters and electric lights—even the chair President Lincoln was sitting in when he was shot. Next stop is the Greenfield Village, where you can visit such places as the Wright brothers' shop, Thomas Edison's laboratory, or ride on an antique carousel.

Alphabet Favorites!
Wow! Look at all of these cool things. Can you find something that begins with each letter of the alphabet.

BE MINE

In the world's largest Children's Museum you can explore a cave, match wits with computers, and conduct scientific experiments. Or, "drive" a real Indy 500 car, whirl on a carousel, and zoom through deep space. Ever wanted to ride a camel? You can at the Indianapolis Zoo.

Indianapolis

Indiana

Race Away!

You will need three different coins to play this game—two to use as markers and one to flip. Flip the coin to determine how many spaces to move—heads, move two spaces; tails move one space. Follow the directions on spaces where you land. First one to the Finish Line take the checkered flag.

START

FINISH

GREEN FLAG MOVE 3 SPACES

LAP LEADER MOVE 3 SPACES

SPIN OUT MOVE 1 SPACE BACK

CAUTION MOVE 1 SPACE

OUT OF GAS LOSE 1 TURN

DEBRIS ON TRACK MOVE 1 SPACE BACK

NEW TIRES EXTRA TURN

FLAT TIRE MOVE 2 SPACES BACK

HIT THE WALL! YOU LOSE

PIT STOP LOSE 1 TURN

Bluegrass Country

Kentucky

Like horses? You'll LOVE Kentucky Horse Park in Lexington. There are all kinds of horsey things to see and do. For horse racing excitement, ride over to the Kentucky Derby Museum in Louisville. Or, take a sternwheeler cruise, learn "The Legend of Daniel Boone," explore a fort, or see Lincoln's birthplace.

Horses, Horses, Horses!

Can you correctly identify these parts of a horse? Fill in the numbers.

Barrel_____   Hoof_____

Chest_____   Mane_____

Fetlock_____   Nostrils_____

Forelock_____   Tail_____

Haunch_____   Thigh_____

Hock_____   Withers_____

How much do you know about horses? True or False?

A newbord horse is a foal._____

A mare is a mother horse._____

All Thoroughbred horses are one year older every January 1st. _____

Horses always sleep lying down._____

Horses were brought to America by the Spaniards. _____

The father of a horse is its sire._____

Ponies are baby horses._____

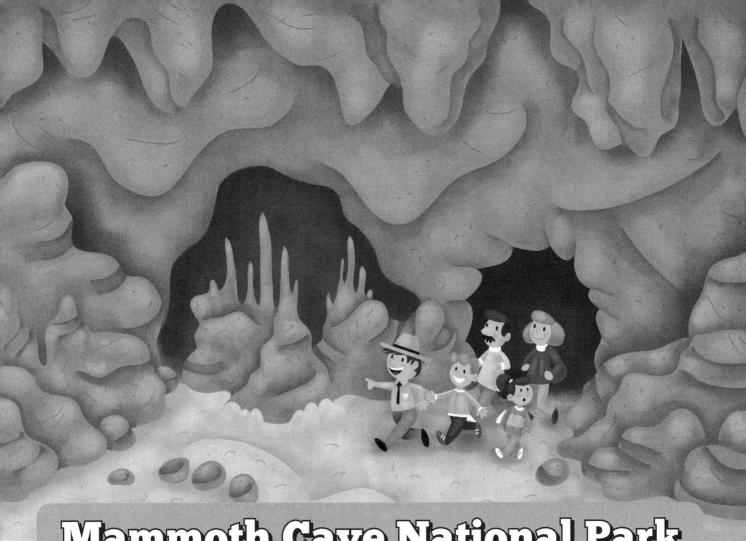

Mammoth Cave National Park

You won't find the Flintstones here, but you will find lots of other "stone age" things, such as a waterfall, icicles, needles, popcorn, snowballs, and flowers. Special sections include Fat Man's Misery, Bottomless Pit, and Mummy Ledge. Oh, don't forget a jacket—caves are really "cool" places.

Kentucky

Black Hills Trivia

Which grows up and which grows down? Stalagmites or Stalactites?

Did you know that many fish in caves are either blind or have no eyes at all?

Caves are formed in limestone rocks by dripping or running water.

Mammoth Cave has more than 330 miles of explored passageways, and it is still growing.

The Snowball Dining Room is 267 feet beneath the surface.

The temperature in the cave is 54°F all year.

Mammoth Cave is the longest known cave system in the world, and there are many other caves in the area.

Bats are in some caves, but they often leave at sundown to eat.

St. Louis

Scrunch into an elevator that looks kind of like a clothes dryer, and ride up Gateway Arch to see the sights. Back on earth, find everything from furry-footed Clydesdale horses to buffalo at Grants Farm. Catch your shadow at the Magic House, or roam the zoo and Science Center in Forest Park.

Missouri

Scrambled States!

It would be fun to visit some of these cool places, but their states are all mixed up. Unscramble the states. Then match each great place with its state.

1. SALAKA _____
2. DORFAIL _____
3. WEN KORY _____
4. FLAIRCOINA _____
5. ZORAINA _____
6. VENSILPANNAY _____
7. SCHATUMASSETS _____
8. THOUS TAKODA _____
9. REGOIGA _____
10. RISOSUMI _____
11. LISINILO _____
12. STOMENANI _____
13. SAXET _____
14. DOOLACOR _____
15. NECKTUYK _____

Alamo _____
Denali _____
Everglades _____
Golden Gate Bridge _____
Grand Canyon _____
Gateway Arch _____
Liberty Bell _____
Mammoth Cave _____
Mount Rushmore _____
Pikes Peak _____
Plymouth Rock _____
Willis Tower _____
Statue of Liberty _____
Stone Mountain _____
10,000 Lakes _____

Skinny, twisting roads roller coaster the Ozark Mountains. At the Ozark Folk Center, see what mountain life was like before there were roads. Spend a day at Silver Dollar City. Ride the rides, listen to country music, watch old-time crafters or tour a cave. Fish and swim at Table Rock Lake, or catch the shows in Branson.

Missouri

Arkansas

Ozarks

Fun Time!

Find and circle these things you can see and do on vacation. Then find the secret message in the leftover letters.

Ball	Merry-go-round
Bike	Museum
Boat	Raft
Bumper cars	Read
Camp	Ride
Cave	Roller coaster
Climb	Row
Drive	Sail
Eat	Sand castles
Ferry	Shop
Fish	Sightsee
Fly	Ski
Golf	Sled
Green	Sleep
Hike	Sports
Horse	Swim
Inner tube	Swing
Lake	Trip
Look	Water park
Maze	Zoo

R	O	W	S	R	A	C	R	E	P	M	U	B
A	O	F	A	E	A	T	M	G	N	I	W	S
F	T	L	I	A	H	A	E	Y	L	F	E	E
T	A	O	L	D	S	T	R	O	P	S	E	L
E	O	G	R	E	E	N	R	V	I	K	S	T
Z	B	E	F	E	R	R	Y	I	I	R	T	S
A	M	U	K	I	I	C	G	B	P	A	H	A
M	I	A	T	D	S	G	O	P	O	P	G	C
U	L	O	E	R	D	H	R	A	E	R	I	D
E	C	O	L	V	E	H	O	R	S	E	S	N
S	A	A	O	L	I	N	U	P	W	T	L	A
U	V	T	M	K	A	R	N	I	I	A	E	S
M	E	M	E	P	E	B	D	I	M	W	D	R

Natchez

Clip-clop through town in a horse-drawn carriage as they did in the old days. Visit Longwood, the largest eight-sided house in the U.S., a beautiful mansion started in 1860 but never finished. Discover the life of the Natchez Indians. Along the Natchez Trace you will find an eerie cypress swamp.

Mississippi

Shapely States!

Many states are shaped like no other state. Can you identify these states just from their shape? Check the map on pages 4 and 5, if you need a hint.

New Orleans

Clap to the music of street performers in the French Quarter. See the Mississippi from a sternwheeler or a ferry. Meet some "finny friends" at the aquarium, or hop on a bell-clanging streetcar to the fabulous zoo. In City Park, boat the lagoons, ride a carousel, or visit Storyland.

Louisiana

Sail Away!
Down the Mississippi River sail two identical sternwheelers—or are they? Can you find 10 differences between them?

Huntsville

Feeling spacey? Head for the U.S. Space and Rocket Center. You can take a bus tour of the NASA labs and shuttle test sites. Try out weightlessness, work hands-on displays, or surround yourself with an Omnimax space exploration film. An outdoor park is filled with a forest of real rockets.

Off to Space!

Rockets sprout like tulips in this rocket park. Follow-the-dots to add a few more, then color the picture.

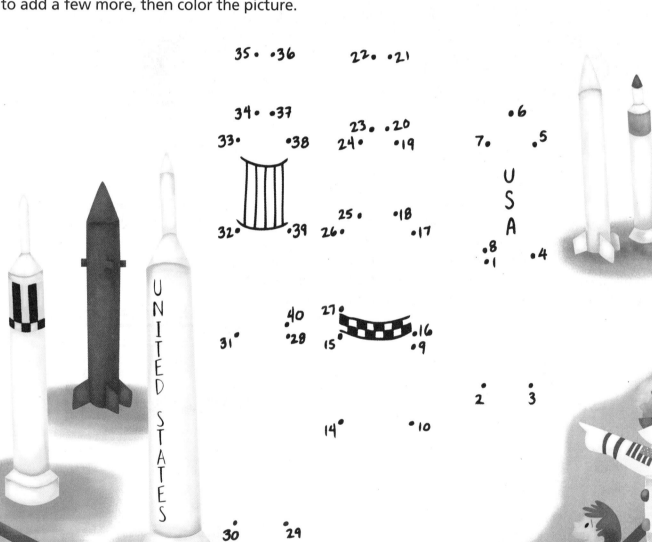

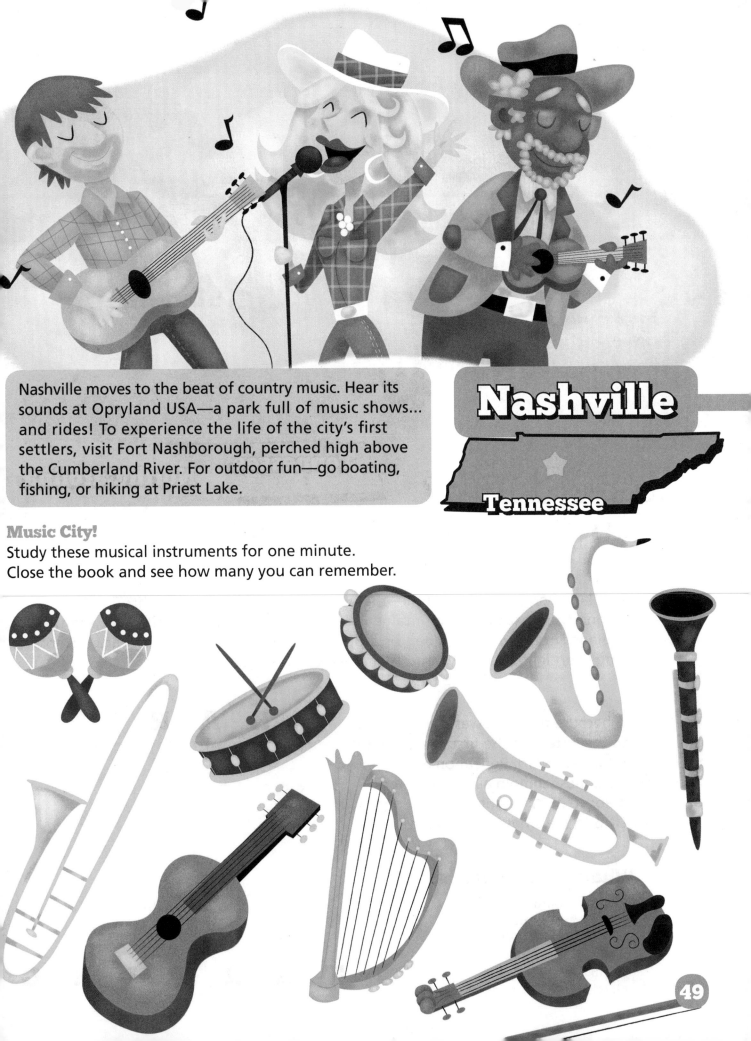

Nashville moves to the beat of country music. Hear its sounds at Opryland USA—a park full of music shows... and rides! To experience the life of the city's first settlers, visit Fort Nashborough, perched high above the Cumberland River. For outdoor fun—go boating, fishing, or hiking at Priest Lake.

Nashville
Tennessee

Music City!
Study these musical instruments for one minute.
Close the book and see how many you can remember.

Great Smoky Mountains National Park

Pull on your hiking boots and hit the trail—the Appalachian Trail. It snakes through the park high along the crest of the mountains. There are lots of shorter trails, too. See the mountain villages in the valleys hidden by bluish mist? That's the "smoke" in Great Smoky. You can camp overnight and Dollywood theme park is nearby.

Hit the Road!

The kids ran because their trip was starting. Add one letter to the letters on the first line, scramble them to form a new word. Repeat on each line. Each new word must contain all of the letters of the word above it. Hint—subtract R, A, and N from STARTING to see what letters to use.

R A N

S T A R T I N G

What's in a Name?

How many words are hiding in the name
GREAT SMOKY MOUNTAINS
(100, maybe 200! No plurals, no proper names)?

50

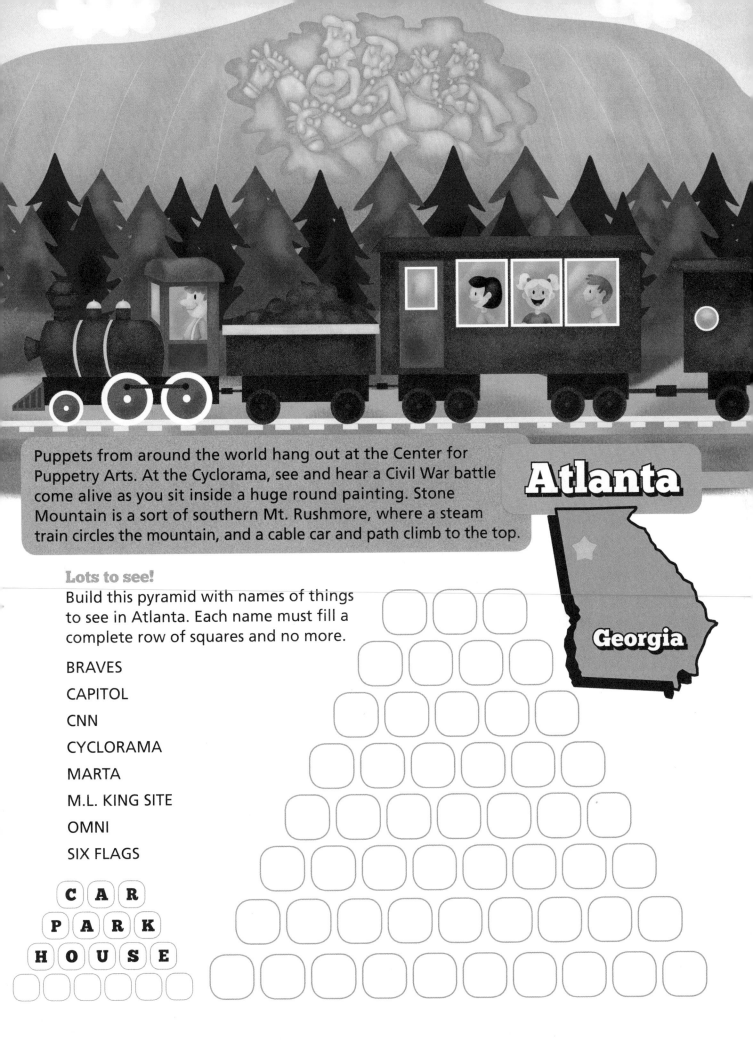

Puppets from around the world hang out at the Center for Puppetry Arts. At the Cyclorama, see and hear a Civil War battle come alive as you sit inside a huge round painting. Stone Mountain is a sort of southern Mt. Rushmore, where a steam train circles the mountain, and a cable car and path climb to the top.

Atlanta

Georgia

Lots to see!

Build this pyramid with names of things to see in Atlanta. Each name must fill a complete row of squares and no more.

BRAVES

CAPITOL

CNN

CYCLORAMA

MARTA

M.L. KING SITE

OMNI

SIX FLAGS

C A R

P A R K

H O U S E

Tampa / St. Petersburg

Florida

Pack your camera and "shoot" your way through an African safari at Busch Gardens. Out on the St. Petersburg pier, you can fish, eat, or shop in an upside-down pyramid. Feel like building a sand castle or body-surfing some waves? Grab a shovel and your suit and head for St. Pete's beaches.

Ahoy Matey!
Shiver me timbers, where's my ship? Connect the dots in order, then color the picture.

52

Everglades National Park

Board an airboat and skim over this "river of grass." Keep a watch out for wildlife. Birds come in many colors—red, blue, pink, white, yellow, and green. Long-legged herons stalk for fish. Alligators and crocodiles lie like floating logs. You may glimpse a shy sea cow (manatee), or see a slithery snake.

Florida

Snakes, pelicans, and gators, oh my!
Can you solve these rebus puzzles about things to see in the Everglades?

GAL. - G + 👁 + 🥞 + ✕

🥄 + YOU OWE $10.00

👩 - H + 🎀 + T

🪚 + 〰️

C + 🌧 ←

T + 👗 ⤵ - SK + L

S N + 🧹 - R

Central Florida / Orlando

Florida

This must be theme park heaven! At Walt Disney World you can meet Mickey Mouse, travel the world, or learn the stunt secrets of Indiana Jones. At Sea World, go eye-to-eye with danger as you walk through a pool of sharks. Then let Universal Studios' earthquake ride *really* shake you up.

What's Up!

What can you find in Central Florida? Solve the sentences below, then fill the right letters in the matching slots at the bottom.

1. Find me in light and toy _____
2. Find me in horse and hug _____
3. Find me in car and ride _____
4. Find me in ice and big _____
5. Find me in log and pile _____
6. Find me in line and luck _____
7. Find me in smile and sad _____

Did You Know?

Central Florida is a fun-filled playground today. Not too long ago it was mostly acres and acres of citrus groves, large cattle ranches, and a few swamps.

I spy!

If you're looking out the window, try to find something that begins with each letter of the alphabet, in order. You can play this game alone or with another traveler.

_____ _____ _____ _____ _____ _____ _____
 1   2   3   4   5   6   7

Nonstop Fun!

Unscramble these great vacation sights in central Florida.

NALROTILAGDAL _____

SPRYCES SNARGED _____

YESNID-GMM DOSITUS _____

CEPTO TENREC _____

LORDIFA RITCUS WROTE _____

ESA DORLW FO DIFROLA _____

LIVERS GRINSPS _____

KRASH COTRENUNE _____

SILVERUNA TOSSIDU RALFIDO _____

TWAL NESDIY DROWL _____

Central Florida

Want more? How about exciting waterski and bird shows at Cypress Gardens? Or Gatorland Zoo—crawling with thousands of huge and small alligators and crocodiles? Ride a glass-bottom boat over rainbow-colored fish. Find your state stone in a monument built of cement and stones from every state.

Cape Canaveral/Titusville

Florida

This is where the space shuttles lift off. Start at the Kennedy Space Center to experience the blast of an imitation countdown and launch—maybe even a real one! See space capsules and space suits. And, hundreds of birds who share their sky with man.

Cape Caper!

Strange things are happening at Cape Canaveral and Merritt Island National Wildlife Refuge. Find ten things that are not quite right.

Some parts of Florida have lived under as many as eight flags, since Europeans arrived in 1513.

St. Augustine

This city is OLD—the oldest in the United States. Cross the moat and climb the ramparts of a 300-year-old fort. Wander the narrow streets to find the oldest house and the oldest wooden school. Watch "Spanish settlers" at work. Stop for a sip at the Fountain of Youth or a dip at the beach.

Florida

Flag facts!

During her history, St. Augustine has lived under four flags. Can you match these flags with their countries?

1513 Spain
1763 England
1783 Spain
1821 United States of America
1861 Confederate States of America
1862 United States of America

Charleston

Explore a five-sided piece of American history, Fort Sumter, where the first shots of the Civil War were fired. At Magnolia Plantation, tread the boardwalks into a swamp garden. At Charles Towne Landing, see a colonial village, sailing ships, and wolves, bears, pumas, and other native wildlife roaming the Animal Forest.

Spot These Sights!

Play Tic-Tac-Toe with Charleston sights. Look for the item (or something sort of like it) pictured in the square you want to play. When you find it put a coin or marker over the picture. Set a limit on how long you can look for the correct item. Each player should use a different type of coin or marker. If you are playing along, see how long it takes you to get three in a row, or to cover the whole board.

Bridge	Garden	Church
Theater	Fort Sumter	Golf Course
Boat	House	Horse and Buggy

Cape Hatteras

North Carolina

Hit the beaches, the water's fine! Go swimming, windsurfing, or deep-sea fishing. Explore skeletons of old shipwrecks. Visit Kitty Hawk and stand on the spot where the first airplane flight took place almost 100 years ago. Try solving the mystery of the Lost Colony.

Who's Idea!

With which inventor or discoverer is each of these items linked?

Alexander Graham Bell _____

George Washington Carver _____

Pierre and Marie Curie _____

George Eastman _____

Thomas Alva Edison _____

Benjamin Franklin _____

Guglielmo Marconi _____

Samuel F.B. Morse _____

Eli Whitney _____

Orville and Wilbur Wright _____

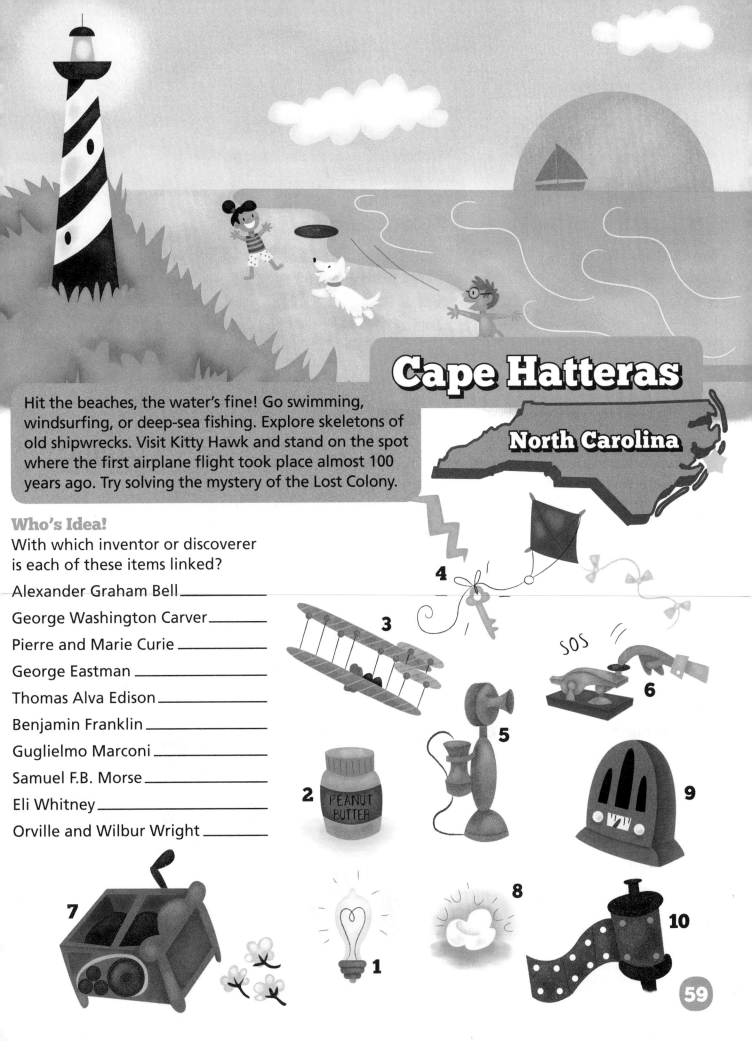

4

3

SOS

6

5

2 PEANUT BUTTER

9

7

8

1

10

Williamsburg

Virginia

A peacock parades across a green common. In the shops, wigs are sewn, barrels are shaped, and teapots are carefully crafted out of fine silver. A wooden stock waits to trap those who misbehave. Men in frock coats visit with women in hoop-skirted dresses. Welcome to Colonial Williamsburg!

You Make What?

Match the historic names of these tradesmen with the items they made. Fill in the proper number after its matching trade.

Apothecary_____

Baker_____

Blacksmith_____

Cabinetmaker_____

Chemist_____

Cooper_____

Milliner_____

Peruke Maker_____

Silversmith_____

Wheelwright_____

4

1

2

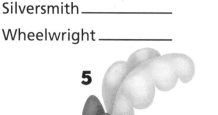
3

9

5

6

7

8

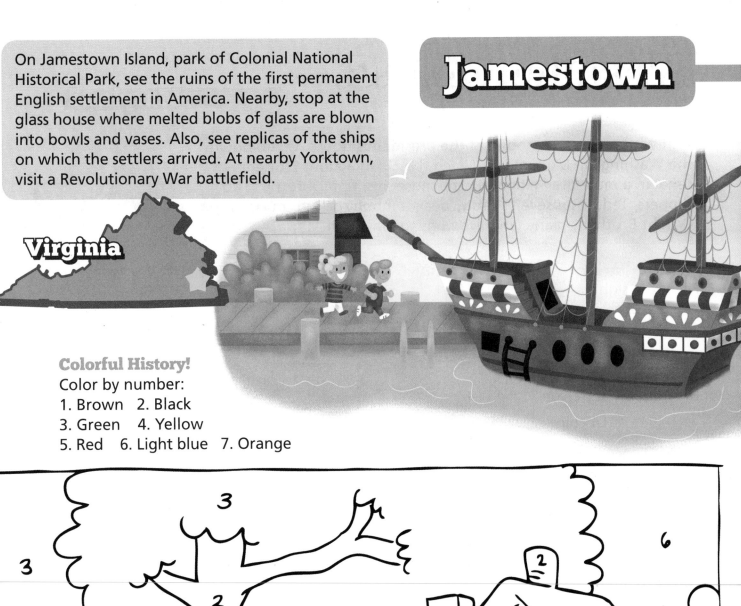

On Jamestown Island, park of Colonial National Historical Park, see the ruins of the first permanent English settlement in America. Nearby, stop at the glass house where melted blobs of glass are blown into bowls and vases. Also, see replicas of the ships on which the settlers arrived. At nearby Yorktown, visit a Revolutionary War battlefield.

Jamestown

Virginia

Colorful History!
Color by number:
1. Brown   2. Black
3. Green   4. Yellow
5. Red   6. Light blue   7. Orange

Washington, D.C.

Maryland

Visit with pandas, or stop in at the president's house. Climb down the Washington Monument. Watch the FBI in action. Cruise a canal in a mule-drawn boat. In the museums, find Dorothy's ruby slippers, Teddy Roosevelt's teddy bear, a moon rock to touch, the Wright Brother's plane, and live bugs to play with.

Oh Say Can You See in Washington, D.C.?
Fill in the sights.

Museums: Freer

Smithsonian

U.S. Holocaust

Memorials: Jefferson

Lincoln

Vietnam Veterans

(The) Wall

Capitol

Congress

FBI

Ford's Theater

Kennedy Center

Mall

Potomac (River)

Supreme Court

Union (Station)

Washington Monument

White House

Wolf Trap

Zoo

Capital Quiz!

How much do you know about our nation's capital? Try this quiz and see.

What is the tallest masonry (stone or brick) structure in the world?

Where do they print money?

What monument has 58,156 names on it?

Where can you find the Wright Brothers' 1903 *Flyer*, Lindbergh's *Spirit of St. Louis*, and the *Apollo* command module?

Where does the president live?

What is found on the land surrounding Robert E. Lee's former home?

What is the "Castle?"

Where can you find a dragon?

Where can you see a panda?

What two letters in American Sign Language do Lincoln's hands form on his statue at the Lincoln Memorial?

Baltimore

Maryland

Rustle through a rain forest, stare down a shark, beware the red-bellied piranha when you enter the National Aquarium. Climb aboard a ship that battled pirates almost 200 years ago. Visit Babe Ruth's birthplace and Ft. McHenry—the site of the battle that inspired the "Star Spangled Banner."

Fancy Fins!

See all of the beautiful fish. Only two of them are alike. Can you find them?

Downtown sits in a "Golden Triangle." Rivers sweep by two sides to form the Ohio River at the triangle's point. Creep steeply up Mount Washington by incline (hill-climbing trolleys) for a great view of all three rivers. Control your own sky trip at the Science Center. Roam Dinosaur Hall at the Natural History Museum.

Pittsburgh

Pennsylvania

Did You Know?

Once dark and dingy from steel mills and mines, today Pittsburgh is a beautiful modern city. It has shining steel and glass buildings, lots of museums, music, and sports.

Solve the Mystery!

How many triangles are hidden in this mysterious pyramid? How many can you find?

Secret clue...some are made up of more than one little triangle!

Lancaster

Pennsylvania

Enter the world of the Amish. Children study in one-room schools. Men have beards and women wear bonnets. See mule-drawn plows and horse-drawn buggies (even ride in one), but no electric lights—or TV! Nearby Hershey has chocolate air, kiss-shaped streetlights, and a fascinating theme park.

Plain or Fancy?

Many Amish people often do not use modern or fancy things. Draw a line to those they would use. Which would they not use?

Valley Forge

Pennsylvania

Gaze out over the beautiful rolling green hills of this national historical park, and try to imagine you're a soldier in the winter of 1777. It is arctic cold. You're hungry and sick. The tiny log hut you share with other soldiers is bare and dark. General Washington makes battle plans in the stone house that is his headquarters. Life was hard at Valley Forge.

Silent Sentinels!

Antique cannons sit silently, reminding us of the hard-fought American Revolution, when we won our freedom. Two are alike. Find them.

Philadelphia

Pennsylvania

This is where America was born. Visit Independence Hall and see the Liberty Bell. At Penn's Landing, board a battleship or squeeze into a submarine. The world's largest "pinball machine" and lots of super science stuff is in the Franklin Institute. America's first zoo has a four-story treehouse to climb!

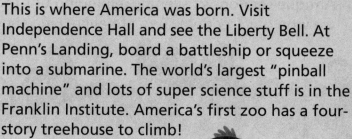

Did You Know?

Philly is famous for...
The Liberty Bell (a must-see for everyone)
Hot pretzels (with or without mustard) sold by corner vendors
Cheese steak sandwiches (a tasty treat)

Did You Know That?

Philadelphia was the home of many famous firsts.

The first U.S. flag, with 13 stars and 13 stripes, was made in Philadelphia. Tradition says, by Betsy Ross.

The first U.S. zoo (1874)

The first Bank of the United States (1797)

The first stock exchange (1790)

The first fire-fighting company (1776)

The first U.S. mint to coin money (1792)

The first daily newspaper (1784)

The first bifocal glasses, invented by Ben Franklin

The first public library (1731)

The first root beer, invented by Charles Hires (1866)

The first ice cream soda (1861)

The first motion picture show in the world (1870)

The first public demonstration of the telephone (1876)

Can You Come Out Even?

As you follow around the square, add and subtract, as directed, the number related to each item listed in the little squares. See if you can come out with the same totals as given at two of the corners.

→ = 1

+ Goldilock's Bears

=

+ Major Oceans (Seas)

=

- Fingers

=

+ Planets

=

- Corners in a square

- Quintet

=

=

- Age to vote

+ U.S. States

=

=

- Original Colonies

- Dozen

=

=

+ Bakers Dozen

- Stripes in U.S. Flag

=

+ Pair

=

- Half Dozen

=

+ Lucky Clover Leaves

=

- Continents

30 =

Niagara Falls

These falls are part American, part Canadian. Peer down on them from a tower almost 300 feet high. For a closer view, head for the island at the edge of the plunging water. For a REALLY close look (you'll get wet) take a boat ride past the base of the falls, or walk right into the spray.

Awesome!
Guide *The Maid of the Mist* safely through the thundering waters back to the pier.

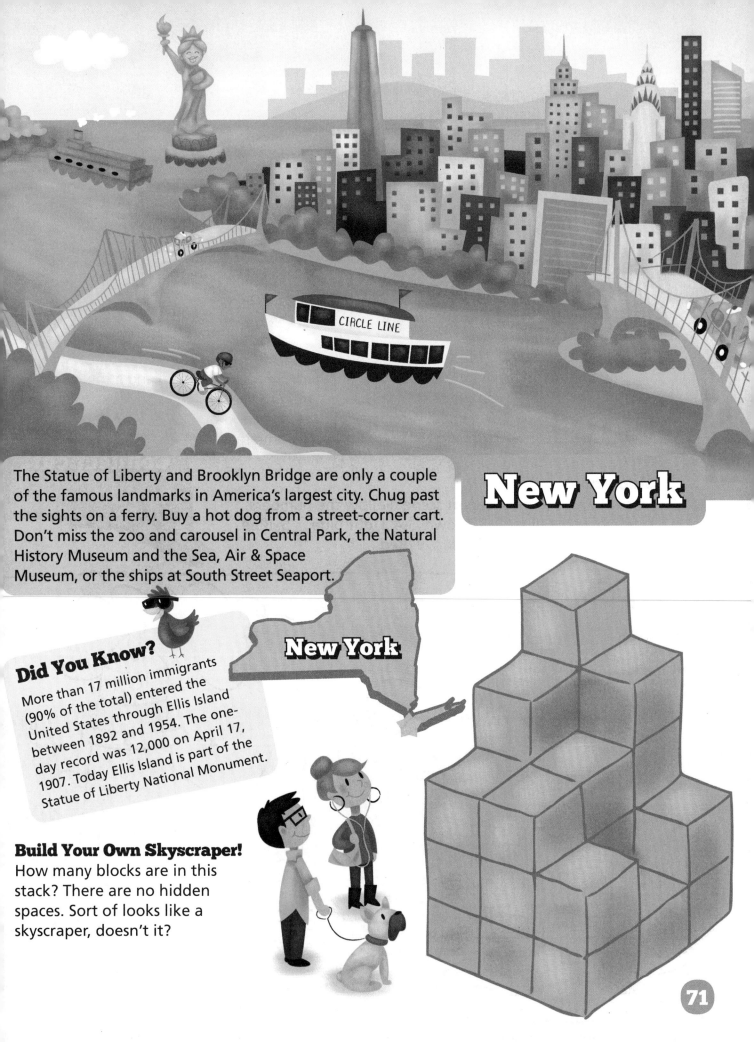

The Statue of Liberty and Brooklyn Bridge are only a couple of the famous landmarks in America's largest city. Chug past the sights on a ferry. Buy a hot dog from a street-corner cart. Don't miss the zoo and carousel in Central Park, the Natural History Museum and the Sea, Air & Space Museum, or the ships at South Street Seaport.

New York

New York

Did You Know?

More than 17 million immigrants (90% of the total) entered the United States through Ellis Island between 1892 and 1954. The one-day record was 12,000 on April 17, 1907. Today Ellis Island is part of the Statue of Liberty National Monument.

Build Your Own Skyscraper!

How many blocks are in this stack? There are no hidden spaces. Sort of looks like a skyscraper, doesn't it?

Mystic

Tall masts creak and sway as ships ride at anchor in an 1800s fishing village. Scramble over the decks of a whaling ship and a square-rigger. Help set a ship's sails. Listen to hammers pound as you watch ships being built. Make rope and learn to tie knots like a sailor. Stop by the nearby aquarium.

Connecticut

Ship Ahoy!
Let's color this Mystic Seaport scene. Follow the numbers.
1. Green   2. Yellow   3. Brown   4. Light blue   5. Blue
6. Gray   7. Purple   8. Black   9. Red

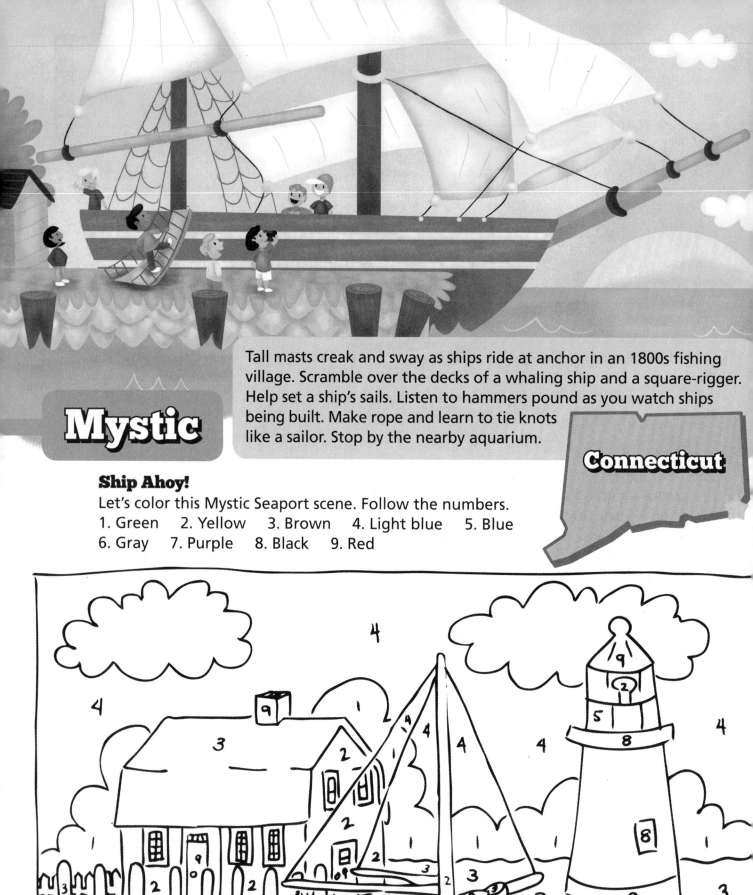

Climb sand dunes and race small shore birds along the beaches. Swim, boat, go fishing, or go whale watching. See an Aqua Circus. Climb Pilgrim Monument tower. Like to bike? There are great bike trails all over Cape Cod. Or, ferry out to Martha's Vineyard or Nantucket for two-wheel island exploring.

Cape Cod
Massachusetts

Chart Challenge!
Match the names of these geographic features with their numbers on the map.

Bay _____   Lake _____

Canal _____   Ocean _____

Cape _____   Peninsula _____

Channel _____   Reservoir _____

Dam _____   River _____

Delta _____   Sound _____

Inlet _____   Tributary _____

Island _____

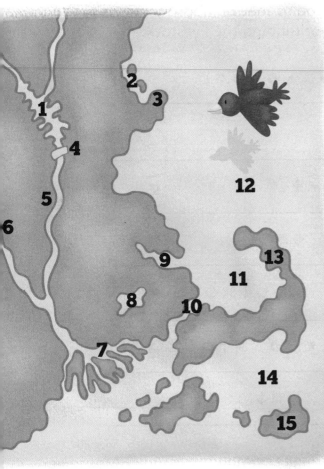

Plymouth

Massachusetts

See Plymouth Rock where the Pilgrims landed in 1620, and explore the small, crowded quarters of a replica of their ship, the *Mayflower.* At Plimoth Plantation, the Pilgrims will take time to chat with you as they go about their daily chores—cooking, mending a roof, gardening, or tending the livestock.

Decode It!
Crack the code to solve these Plymouth sights.

A = ◆   N = ✿
B = ✳   O = ↑
C = ✓   P = ▼
D = △   Q = ☽
E = ◇   R = ☆
F = ✕   S = □
G = ■   T = ▲
H = ○   U = ↓
I = ✴   V = ❖
J = ●   W = ✧
K = ✚   X = ✦
L = ▽   Y = →
M = ⌘   Z = ←

▼ ▽ ✳ ⌘ ↑ ▲ ○   ▼ ▽ ◆ ✿ ▲ ◆ ▲ ✳ ↑ ✿
_____

⌘ ◆ → ✕ ▽ ↑ ✧ ◇ ☆
_____

▼ ▽ → ⌘ ↑ ↓ ▲ ○   ✿ ↑ ✓ ✚
_____

▼ ✳ ▽ ■ ✿ ✳ ⌘   ❖ ✳ ▽ ▽ ◆ ■ ◇
_____

✕ ↑ ☆ ◇ ✕ ◆ ▲ ○ ◇ ☆ □   ⌘ ↑ ✿ ↓ ⌘ ◇ ✿ ▲
_____

⌘ → ▽ ◇ □   □ ▲ ◆ ✿ △ ✳ □ ○   ⌘ ↑ ✿ ↓ ⌘ ◇ ✿ ▲
_____

▼ ✳ ▽ ■ ✿ ✳ ⌘   ○ ◆ ▽ ▽   ⌘ ↓ □ ◇ ↓ ⌘
_____

↑ ▽ △   ✕ ↑ ☆ ▲   ○ ↑ ↓ □ ◇
_____

Boston

Massachusetts

Look down, find the red marks...then walk your way through history. Peek into Paul Revere's house, visit John Hancock's grave, tread the decks of "Old Ironsides." Go modern at a hands-on Computer Museum. Visit the four-story aquarium, ride a swan boat, or eat at the Quincy Market food stalls.

Follow the Freedom Trail!

The green brick line leads to history. The trail is 3 miles long. Here are the highlights.

1 **Begin at Boston Common–**
Oldest U.S. public park

2 **State House and Archives (1795)**

3 **Park Street Church (1809)**
Gun powder factory, War of 1812

4 **Granary Burying Ground**
John Hancock, Samuel Adams and Paul Revere are buried here

5 **King's Chapel (1754)**

6 **First Public School Site (1635)**
and Benjamin Franklin statue

7 **Old Corner Bookstore (1712)**
Famous authors met here

8 **Old South Meeting House (1729)**
Boston Tea Party began here

9 **Old State House (1713)**
Now Museum of Boston History

10 **Boston Massacre Site**
British soldiers fought colonists

11 **Faneuil Hall (1742)**
Called "the Cradle of Liberty"

12 **Paul Revere House (ca. 1680)**
Oldest Structure in Boston

13 **Old North Church-Christ Church (1723)**
City's oldest church still in use. In April 1775, lanterns in the steeple warned of the British coming—one if by land; two if by sea

14 **Copp's Hill Burial Ground (1660)**

15 **U.S.S. Constitution ("Old Ironsides")**
Oldest commissioned U.S. warship afloat; also museum

16 **Bunker Hill Monument**
Battle on June 17, 1775

U.S.S. Constitution

Boston Harbor

Old State House

Bunker Hill Monument

Adams
Chelsea
Water
Main
Charlestown Bridge
Commercial
Causeway
Prince
Hull
John F. Fitzgerald Expressway
Salem
Hanover
North
Richmond
New Congress
Union
Court
State
Beacon
School
Province
Washington
Milk
Congress
Tremont

Acadia National Park

Maine

Acadia National Park, located mostly on an island, is full of the sounds and sights of the sea. Salty waves crash against tumbled, rocky cliffs and boom into Thunder Hole. Whales slide by, and lobster boats haul in the day's catch. Sailboats dart with the wind. Climb 1,530-foot Cadillac Mountain. Take a cold ocean swim.

Rocky Hideaway!
Find 6 secret objects along the rugged coast of Maine.

Answers

Page 7

Cinder cone	5	Lava	3
Crater	1	Magma	2
Eruption	6	Vent	8
Gas and ash	7	Volcanic bombs	4

Page 8

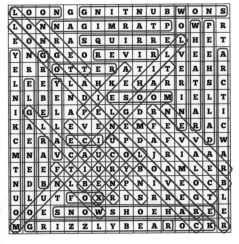

Page 11

Gum wrapper	1 month
Orange peel	3 months
Pop can	200-500 years
Styrofoam cup	Over 500 years
Rubber tire	Over 500 years
Plastic pop rings	Over 500 years
Glass bottle	1,000,000 years

Page 12

Black bear	Antelope
Geysers	Bighorn sheep
Bison	Yellowstone Falls
Mammoth Hot Springs	Bald Eagle
Grizzly bear	Old Faithful
Moose	Paint Pots
Elk (Wapiti)	Beaver

Page 13

Stream	Bread
Table	Bed
Potato	Violin, guitar
Garden	Macaroni, sink pipe
Chair	Cypress tree
Clock	Corn
Wristwatch	Gloves
River	

Page 14

```
            G O L F
I C E S K A T E
        S K I
    R I D E
            T E N N I S
        S A I L
        H I K E
        B O A T
W A T E R S K I
```

Page 15

12 states

New York	Indiana	Wyoming
New Jersey	Illinois	Utah
Pennsylvania	Iowa	Nevada
Ohio	Nebraska	California

Page 16

```
            C       A H W A H N E E
M E A D O W         A           E
E       N       S       L       E
R   Y O S E M I T E F A L L S
C   O       E       D       C
F E R N     Q       R     P A S S
D       U       R O A M   P
    C   O       A     E   H I K E
M A R I P O S A           T   D
    M   A               L A   Y
    P       M O U N T A I N   T
T R A I L           K       H
O       N   T U O L U M N E   V A L E
C       G   R           U     I
K           E A G L E   T   P E A K
            E               W
```

Page 17

The middle section in the left column matches the bottom section in the right column.

Ages of trees:	8	10
	11	6
	7	11

Page 18

CARAMEL	CAROUSEL
CARAWAY	CARPENTER
CARBURETOR	CARPET
CARDS	CARRIAGE
CARDINAL	CARROT
CAREFUL	CARTON
CARNIVAL	

Page 19

Disneyland
Knott's Berry Farm
Hollywood
Farmer's Market
Sea World
Rancho La Brea Tar Pits
Hollywood Bowl
Six Flags Magic Mountain
Universal Studios Hollywood
Queen Mary
Beverly Hills
Rose Bowl
Gene Autry Western Heritage Museum
NBC Studios
Griffith Park Observatory
The Coliseum

Page 20

Giraffe	Lion	Kangaroo
Elephant	Zebra	Hippopotamus
Cheetah	Monkey	

Page 21

1. Indianapolis, Oklahoma City
2. Annapolis, Maryland
3. Baton Rouge (Louisiana)
4. Lincoln, Nebraska
5. Nashville, Tennessee
6. Dover, Delaware; Honolulu,

Hawaii; Indianapolis, Indiana; Oklahoma City, Oklahoma

7. Juneau, Alaska (Honolulu, Hawaii can be reached by car from other parts of Oahu Island)

8. Sacramento, California; Saint Paul, Minnesota; Salem, Oregon; Salt Lake City, Utah; Santa Fe, New Mexico; Springfield, Illinois

9. Santa Fe, New Mexico; established in 1610

10. Pierre (South Dakota)

Page 22

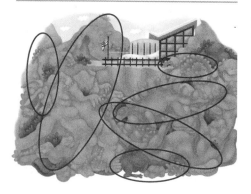

Page 23

```
E  K  C  L  I  F  F
K  C  A  M  P  O  T
I  O  N  W  A  L  L
B  R  Y  C  E  D  O
Z  I  O  N  D  E  R
S  U  N  H  I  K  E
T  O  W  E  R  I  M
```

Page 24

Dam	Clocks	Ring	Bike
Lamb	Blocks	Sing or Swing	Hike
Feet	Light	Mouth	Jump
Beet	Fight	South	Pump
Ball		Book	
Mall		Cook	

Page 25

Page 26

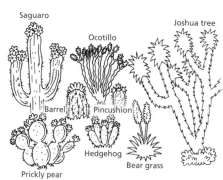

Saguaro • Ocotillo • Joshua tree • Barrel • Pincushion • Hedgehog • Bear grass • Prickly pear

Page 27

Arizona-Sonora Desert Museum	5
Barrio Historico	7
Fort Huachuca	4
Kitt Peak Observatory	1
O.K. Corral	3
Old Tucson	6
Pima Air Museum	2
Tombstone	8

Page 29

Page 31

Trees	Triangle (fire)	Totem
TeePee	Tribesman	Tumbleweed
Tentpoles	Torch	Thistle
Tear	Teeth	Tongue
Toad	Thumb	Tail
Tracks	Tomahawk	Travois
Tom-tom	Toe	Turtle

Page 33

arbol	10	tree
burro	6	donkey
casa	1	house
gato	5	cat
iglesia	3	church, mission
mano	13	hand
niña	12	girl
niño	15	boy
pelo	11	hair
pelota	14	ball
perro	4	dog
piñata	9	candy-filled toy
serape	8	shawl
sol	2	sun
sombrero	7	hat
zapatos	16	shoes

Page 34

Pan	Pickaxe	Shovel
Burro	Miner	Bag of gold

Page 36

Minnesota	Wisconsin
Iowa	Illinois
Missouri	Kentucky
Arkansas	Tennessee
Louisiana	Mississippi

Page 37

Tube 2

Page 38

Bird	Worm
Dog	Bone
Rabbit	Carrot
Bear	Fish
Otter	Shellfish
Giraffe	Leaves
Ape	Banana
Elephant	Peanuts

Page 39

Man with a pack	Lake Huron
Cucumber	Lake Michigan
Wolf head	Lake Superior

Page 40

A	Apple	N	Necklace
B	Ball	O	Orange
C	Candy (sucker)	P	Pail (and shovel)
D	Doll	Q	Quoits
E	Elephant	R	Race car
F	Flashlight	S	Sled
G	Goldfish	T	Tom-tom
H	Hobbyhorse	U	Unicycle
I	Ice cream	V	Valentine
J	Jet (airplane)	W	Wristwatch
K	Keys	X	Xylophone
L	Locomotive	Y	Yo-yo
M	Mitt	Z	Zebra

Page 42

Parts of a horse:

Barrel	7
Chest	10
Fetlock	8
Forelock	12
Haunch	3
Hock	5
Hoof	9
Mane	1
Nostrils	11
Tail	4
Thigh	6
Withers	2

True or false:
T F T F T T F

Page 44

1. Alaska	13		Alamo
2. Florida	1		Denali
3. New York	2		Everglades
4. California	4		Golden Gate Bridge
5. Arizona	5		Grand Canyon
6. Pennsylvania	10		Gateway Arch
7. Massachusetts	6		Liberty Bell
8. South Dakota	15		Mammoth Cave
9. Georgia	8		Mount Rushmore
10. Missouri	14		Pikes Peak
11. Illinois	7		Plymouth Rock
12. Minnesota	11		Willis Tower
13. Texas	3		Statue of Liberty
14. Colorado	9		Stone Mountain
15. Kentucky	12		10,000 Lakes

Page 45

Message: Have a good time

Page 46

Left to right:
Top row — Idaho, Nebraska, Illinois, West Virginia, New Hampshire
Row 2 — California, Texas, Mississippi, Florida

Page 47

Paddlewheel
Flag on prow
Smokestack
Flag on pilot house
First deck 3rd window from right
Second deck near window
Second deck railing
Windows on pilot house
Color of flag on stern

Page 50

These are two possible answers:

RAN	RAN
RAIN	RANG
TRAIN	GRANT
STRAIN	GRANTS
STARING	RATINGS
STARTING	STARTING

Page 51

CNN
OMNI
MARTA
BRAVES
CAPITOL
SIX FLAGS
CYCLORAMA
M.L. KING SITE

Page 53

Alligators
Spoonbill
Airboat
Sawgrass
Crane
Turtle
Snake

Page 54

THRILLS

Page 55

Alligatorland
Cypress Gardens
Disney-MGM Studios
Epcot Center
Florida Citrus Tower
Sea World of Florida
Silver Springs
Shark Encounter
Universal Studios Florida
Walt Disney World

Page 56

Upside down:
Pelican
Rocket
Space Shuttle
Turtle
Swimming duck
Rocket fin
Astronaut on outside of rocket
Heron sitting on rocket
Fish swimming on land
Cattails growing on bottom of stems

Page 57

Flags:
Top row: United States, Confederate States of America
Bottom row: England, Spain

Page 59

Alexander Graham Bell Telephone	5
George Washington Carver Peanut products	2
Pierre and Marie Curie Radium	8
George Eastman Roll film for cameras	10
Thomas Alva Edison Electric lights	1

Benjamin Franklin   4
    Electricity
Guglielmo Marconi   9
    Radio
Samuel F.B. Morse   6
    Telegraph, Morse Code
Eli Whitney   7
    Cotton gin
Orville and Wilbur Wright   3
    Airplane (sustained flight)

Page 60

Apothecary	7	Medicine
Baker	4	Pie
Blacksmith	2	Horseshoe
Cabinetmaker	9	Chair
Chemist	7	Medicine
Cooper	3	Barrel
Milliner	6	Hat, bonnet
Peruke maker	5	Wig
Silversmith	8	Candlestick
Wheelwright	1	Wheel

Page 62

(crossword answers)
CAPITOL, WOLFTRAP, MALL, WASHINGTON, FBI, USHOLOCAUST, SMITHSONIAN, ZOO, CONGRESS, JEFFERSON, WALL, VIETNAMVETERANS, FREER, UNION, POTOMAC

Page 63

Washington Monument
Bureau of Engraving and Printing
Vietnam Veterans' Memorial
National Air & Space Museum
The White House
Arlington National Cemetery
Smithsonian Institution (main building)
Chinatown
National Zoological Park
A and L

Page 64

Page 65

40 triangles

Page 66

Would use:
    candle
    plain coat and hat
    mule and plow
    buggy
    button
    plain dress
Would not use:
    Automobile
    Zipper
    Electricity
    Electric lamp
    Telephone
    Camera

Page 67

The second and fourth cannons from the left match

Page 69

3	bears
7	oceans
10	fingers
9	planets
5	quintet
50	U.S. states
12	dozen
13	flag stripes
7	continents
4	lucky clover leaves
6	half dozen
2	pair
13	baker's dozen
13	original colonies
18	age to vote
4	corners in a square

Page 70

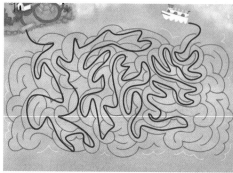

Page 71

27 blocks

Page 73

Bay	11
Canal	10
Cape	13
Channel	2
Dam	4
Delta	7
Inlet	9
Island	15
Lake	8
Ocean	12
Peninsula	3
Reservoir	1
River	5
Sound	14
Tributary	6

Page 74

Plimoth Plantation
Mayflower
Plymouth Rock
Pilgrim Village
Forefathers' Monument
Myles Standish Monument
Pilgrim Hall Museum
Old Fort House

Page 76

Canoe on the shore
Sailboat in the clouds
Moose head in the water
Lobster, fish, and clam in the rocks